Usborne Spotter's Guides

Animals,
Tracks & Signs

Alfred Leutscher

Illustrated by Chris Shields

Consultant: Harry Pepper,
from The Tree Advice Trust

Usborne Quicklinks

The Usborne Quicklinks Website is packed with thousands of links to all the best websites on the internet. The websites include information, video clips, sounds, games and animations that support and enhance the information in Usborne internet-linked books.

To visit the recommended websites for Spotter's Animals, Tracks and Signs, go to the Usborne Quicklinks Website at **www.usborne-quicklinks.com** and enter the keywords: **spotters tracks**

Internet safety

When using the internet please follow the internet safety guidelines displayed on the Usborne Quicklinks Website. The recommended websites in Usborne Quicklinks are regularly reviewed and updated, but Usborne Publishing Ltd is not responsible for the content or availability of any website other than its own. We recommend that children are supervised while using the internet.

Usborne Publishing is not responsible and does not accept liability for the availability or content of any website other than its own, or for any exposure to harmful, offensive, or inaccurate material which may appear on the Web. Usborne Publishing will have no liability for any damage or loss caused by viruses that may be downloaded as a result of browsing the sites it recommends.

Contents

How to use this book

This book will show you many of the mammals, birds and insects that live in Britain and Europe, and also how to identify the signs they leave behind. Their tracks, leftovers, nests and burrows can be easier to find than the animals themselves.

Species

Each different kind of animal is called a species. The descriptions next to each picture tell you what details to look for, where you are likely to find the species and how big it might be.

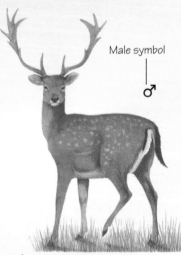

Male symbol

♂

Tracks

All the mammals and birds have an outline of their track next to them. An average size is given for each track.

Mallard

Any webbing between animals' toes is shown in yellow.

The darker the area, the harder the part of the foot.

8cm

Male and female

The males and females of some species are different from each other. The symbols male ♂ and female ♀ show you which is which.

Name and description of species

◀ Fallow deer

Lives in herds in parks and woods. Fawns are born in June with spotted coats. Eats herbs, grass, berries, acorns and leaves. 1m.

Average size

What lives where?

The animals in this book can be found in the areas shown in dark green on this map. A few of the species may be very rare where you live. They may be common in other European countries, though, so you might have a chance to spot them if you go abroad.

Scandinavia

The British Isles

Mainland Europe

Keeping a record

There's an empty circle next to each picture. Whenever you spot an animal or sign for the first time, you can put a tick in the circle.

Species (name)	Score	Date spotted
Cormorant	10	24/05
Coypu	20	
Curlew	15	14/07

You can fill in the scorecard like this.

Scorecard

At the end of the book is a scorecard, which gives you an idea of how common each species and sign is. A common type scores 5 points and a rare one 25. You can add up your score after a day out spotting.

5

Measurements

The animals in this book are not drawn to scale, but the captions or descriptions next to the pictures tell you their size. Here you can see how they are measured.

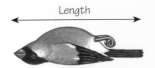

Length

Birds: length of bird from beak to tip of tail, in centimetres

Hoofed mammals: shoulder height in metres or centimetres

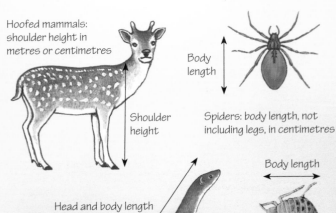

Shoulder height

Body length

Spiders: body length, not including legs, in centimetres

Body length

Head and body length

Other mammals: length of head and body, not including tail, in centimetres

Insects: body length, not including antennae, in centimetres or millimetres

Respecting nature

When out and about in the countryside, always remember to follow this code:

• Never light fires
• Keep to the paths, and close gates behind you
• Keep dogs under control
• Don't damage hedges, fences, walls or signs
• Look, don't touch: leave plants, animals and nests alone
• Take your litter home with you

Looking for tracks and signs

Being prepared

It's best to wear layers of light, waterproof clothing when exploring. You can take this book with you, to help you identify the things you find, and also a notebook and pencils, to jot down what you see. If you have a camera, you could use it to take pictures of the tracks and signs you spot. You could also use binoculars to look at tree tops, watching for birds and their nests.

Through binoculars, you might spot a bird, like this crossbill, snacking in a tree top.

Places to look

• On the lower rung of gates and fences for fur
• In muddy and sandy places for tracks
• Under trees and bushes for fruit and nuts
• On tree bark for peeling and scrape marks
• In grassy areas for paths made by animals
• In front of burrows for tracks

Tracks and trails

A track is an animal's footprint and a trail is a series of tracks made by a moving animal. Finding a trail can not only give you clues to the type of animal that made it, but also where it was going and how it was moving.

This is a fox trail. There's only a single line of footprints, showing that the fox was trotting along, placing its back feet in the prints made by its front feet.

Direction of travel

These prints belong to a running hare. As it ran, it leapt into the air, landing on its front feet first. Then, it put its back feet down a little way in front before leaping again.

A blackbird usually hops, but can break into a run if it senses danger. These tracks are paired, so you can tell that the blackbird that left them was hopping along calmly.

Wading birds, like this curlew, leave trails as they pace up and down muddy shores looking for food.

Making casts

The tracks shown in this book are complete, but the ones you find may have parts missing or be misshapen by thawing snow or uneven ground. If you spot a perfect, deep print in firm ground, you can make a plaster cast of it to keep as a permanent record of your find.

To make a plaster cast you'll need:

- quick-drying plaster of Paris from a craft shop
- a strip of cardboard 30cm x 5cm
- lip balm
- a paper clip
- a container
- an old spoon
- water

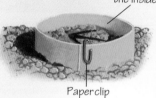

Lip balm on the inside

Paperclip

1. Smear lip balm on one side of the cardboard. Bend the cardboard around the print, clipping the ends together to form a ring.

2. Press the ring into the soil. Using the spoon, mix some plaster in the container, as directed on the packet, then pour it into the ring.

Plaster

3. Leave it to set for about 20 minutes. Gently lift up the plaster cast.

Deer

➡ Red deer

Lives in herds in open country and woods. In winter, the males and females separate into two herds. Young have spotted coats. Eats grass, fruit, heather and tree bark. May raid crops. 1.5m.

Red-brown summer coat

8cm

7cm

♂

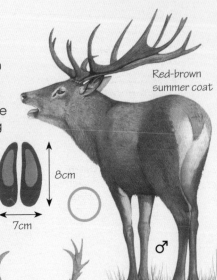

5cm

6.3cm

Flattened, palm-shaped antlers

♂

⬅ Fallow deer

Lives in herds in parks and woods. Fawns are born in June with spotted coats. Eats herbs, grass, berries, acorns and leaves. 1m.

Black lines running down forehead

3cm

➡ Muntjac

Lives on its own or in pairs, in thick undergrowth in woods. Quiet, but barks if frightened. Eats mainly bramble and wild herbs. 50cm.

♂

➡ Roe deer

Red-brown in summer, grey-brown in winter. Lives on its own or in small family groups in woods. Eats leaves, herbs and berries. 70cm.

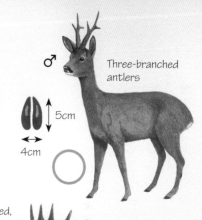

Three-branched antlers

5cm
4cm

16cm

Flattened, palm-shaped antlers

12cm

⬅ Elk / moose

Largest European deer. Found in woods or marshes in northern and eastern Europe. Not found in Britain. Lives on its own in summer, and in herds in winter. Swims well. Eats water plants, grass and moss. 1.8m.

Beard

Usually only four branches on each antler

5cm
8cm

➡ Sika deer

Originally from Asia. Females live in small groups. Males are solitary. Eats heather and grass. May raid crops. 80cm.

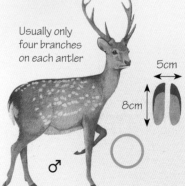

Deer and sheep

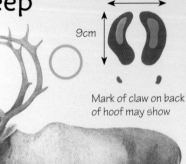

9cm

9cm

Mark of claw on back
of hoof may show

➡ Reindeer

Both sexes have antlers.
Coat colour varies.
Lives in herds
in mountains
and tundra
of northern
Scandinavia.
A herd has been
introduced to
Scotland. Eats grass,
heather and lichen. 1.1m.

Curved, spiral horns

5cm

4cm

◀ Mouflon / wild sheep

Ancestor of domestic sheep.
Mainly nocturnal. Lives in
small flocks in open mountain
woods. Not found in Britain.
Eats grass, moss, buds and
berries. 70cm.

Rounded ends

6cm

5cm

➡ Domestic sheep

Many different breeds.
Kept in fields, open
pastures, or mountains.
Lives in flocks with an
old female as leader.
Eats mainly grass. Size
varies with breed.

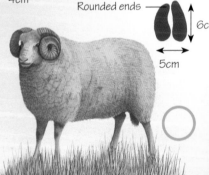

Goats and chamois

➡ Domestic goat

Many different breeds. Most are domesticated on farms, but some roam wild on mountains. Male usually has a beard. Size varies with breed.

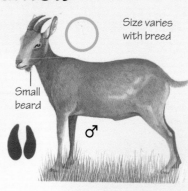

Size varies with breed

Small beard

♂

Similar to sheep tracks

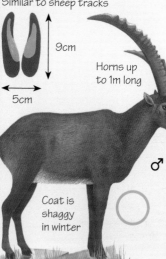

9cm

5cm

Horns up to 1m long

Coat is shaggy in winter

♂

⬅ Ibex / wild goat

Lives in flocks on high mountains in Europe. Not found in Britain. Male has a beard. Very agile. Eats grass, lichen, moss and leaves. 75cm.

3.5cm

6cm

Brown coat turns grey in winter

➡ Chamois

Both sexes have horns. Lives in flocks on wooded mountains. Not found in Britain. Males live on their own. Very agile. Eats grass, berries and buds. 75cm.

Cows, pigs and ponies

➡ Domestic cow

Colour and size vary
with breed. Some
have horns. Cows
bred for beef can
be seen roaming on
moors and mountains.

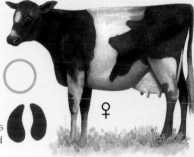

♀

Size varies
with breed

7cm

Claw

Stiff,
bristly fur

⬅ Wild boar

Ancestor of domestic pig.
Lives in woods and marshes
of Europe. Very rare in
Britain. Males are solitary,
females live in small groups.
Eats roots, bark, and fallen
fruit such as acorns. 90cm.

➡ Domestic pig

Size and colour vary
with breed. Kept
mainly on farms, but
can be kept as pets.
Omnivorous.

Size
varies
with
breed

⬅ Exmoor pony

Lives semi-wild in herds on
Exmoor. There are no othe
semi-wild ponies in Britain.
Eats grass, leaves and
low-growing plants. 1.3m.

Track is made by one toe

Wolves, dogs and bears

➡ Wolf

Usually lives on its own
in remote forests in
Spain, Scandinavia,
Italy and Eastern
Europe. In winter,
lives in packs.
Hunts silently
for deer. 1.2m.

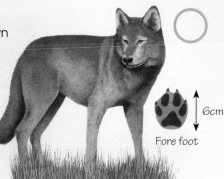

6cm

Fore foot

Size varies
with breed

Fore
foot

⬅ Domestic dog

Size and colour vary
with breed. Alsatians
and huskies look
similar to wolves.
Eats mainly meat.

Fore foot   Hind foot

30cm

20cm

➡ Brown bear

Usually lives on its own
in remote areas of Europe.
Not found in Britain.
Nocturnal. Hibernates
in caves in winter.
Omnivorous. 2m.

Foxes and badgers

➡ Red fox

Common on farmland and in woods, but also found on mountains and in towns. Usually nocturnal. Hunts and scavenges mammals, birds and insects. 65cm.

Small pad

6cm

5cm

Fore foot Hind foot

⬅ Arctic fox

Lives on tundra and mountains in northern Scandinavia. Not found in Britain. Coat is dull brown in summer; usually all white in winter, occasionally grey. Lives in small groups. Active by day and night. 60cm.

Winter coat

Tracks are 4.5cm, and similar to those of the red fox

➡ Badger

Found mainly in woods, but also on mountains. Nocturnal. Lives in a large group, in networks of tunnels called setts. Eats mainly worms; also small mammals, insect larvae, wasp nests, cereals and roots. 80cm.

Kidney shaped pad

4cm

5cm

Fore foot Hind foot

Stoats, weasels, mink and polecats

➡ Stoat

Found in woods, farmland and on mountains. Northern stoats, called ermines, are white in winter. Tip of tail is always black. Eats rabbits, small rodents, birds and eggs. 28cm.

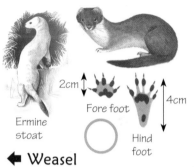

Ermine stoat

2cm

Fore foot

4cm

Hind foot

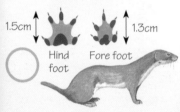

1.5cm

Hind foot

1.3cm

Fore foot

➡ European mink

Native to France and Eastern Europe. American mink have escaped from fur farms in Britain and Europe. Lives near water and swims well. Stores food in its den. Eats fish, frogs, rabbits and birds. 38cm.

Hind foot

5cm

Fore foot

3cm

Dark marks on face

⬅ Weasel

Lives in similar areas to stoats; prefers dry places. Not found in Ireland. Nocturnal. Runs with an arched back. Eats small mammals and birds. 20cm.

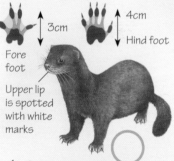

3cm

Fore foot

4cm

Hind foot

Upper lip is spotted with white marks

⬅ Polecat

Nocturnal. Found in wooded country, often near houses. Tame polecats are called ferrets. Eats rabbits, frogs, birds and rodents. 40cm.

Otters and martens

➡ Otter

Found along marshes, rivers, lakes, and coastal areas, and on offshore islands. Lives on its own. Nocturnal. Expert swimmer. Eats fish, crabs, eels, frogs, waterfowl and rabbits. 70cm.

Powerful tail, called a rudder

Hind foot Fore foot

5cm

6cm

⬅ Pine marten

Shy and nocturnal. Lives in mountain woods, usually amongst conifer trees. Good climber. Eats insects, berries, small mammals and birds. 50cm.

Fore foot Hind foot

6cm

5.5cm

Yellow patch

Bushy tail

Feet are furry underneath

White patch

➡ Beech marten

Lives in woods and on farmland, often close to houses. Not found in Britain. Climbs well. Eats small mammals, birds and sometimes fruit. 45cm.

Fore foot

5cm

Hind foot

4.5cm

Cats

➡ Domestic cat

Many different breeds. Fed by people, but often hunts small mammals and birds. Active by day and night. Size varies with breed.

Size varies with breed

No claw marks

Fore foot Hind foot

Broad head

Bushy tail with blunt black tip

⬅ Wild cat

Found in remote, woody areas, or among rocks in Scotland and Europe. Nocturnal and shy. Eats mountain animals, such as hares, small deer, small rodents and grouse. 65cm.

Hind foot   6cm

Fore foot

➡ Lynx

Lives in remote mountain woods in Scandinavia and Eastern Europe. Nocturnal and solitary. Eats deer, hares, and game birds. 1.1m.

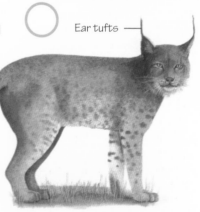

Ear tufts

Short tail

Hind foot Fore foot

8cm   7cm

Beavers, coypu and muskrats

➡ Beaver

Small colonies can be seen in Europe. Builds a dam in a river or lake. Families live in a lodge, a large conical pile of branches. Eats water plants, bark and roots of aspen, willow and poplar trees. 85cm.

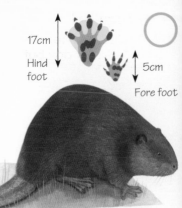

17cm
Hind foot

5cm
Fore foot

Webbed feet

⬅ Coypu

Originally from South America. Has escaped from fur farms in Europe. Not found in Britain. Lives beside water, burrowing into the banks. Eats waterside plants and root crops. 59cm.

Webbed hind feet

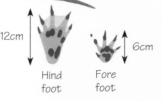

12cm

Hind foot

6cm

Fore foot

The sides of the tail are flattened

➡ Muskrat

Lives beside fresh water. Has escaped from fur farms in Europe. Not found in Britain. Eats waterside plants. 33cm.

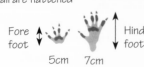

Fore foot

Hind foot

5cm   7cm

Squirrels and dormice

➡ Red squirrel

Lives mostly in conifer woods. Active by day, but shy. Eats seeds of cones, berries, buds, birds' eggs, nuts and fungi. 23cm.

Fore foot
3cm

Hind foot
4cm

Ear tufts

Hind foot
4cm

Fore foot
3cm

⬅ Grey squirrel

Similar habits to red squirrel, but is more common and less shy. Found in parks, gardens and woods. Eats seeds, acorns and nuts. 27cm.

➡ Edible dormouse

Native to Europe and Asia. Not found in Scotland. Found in deciduous woods, parks, and orchards. May live near houses. Nocturnal. Hibernates in winter. Eats nuts, fruit, insects, flowers, pollen and bark. 12cm.

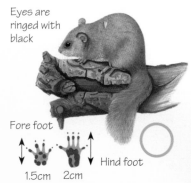

Eyes are ringed with black

Fore foot

1.5cm 2cm

Hind foot

21

Dormice and hamsters

➡ Common dormouse

Lives in woods and hedges. Uses honeysuckle bark to build its hibernation and breeding nests. Nocturnal and solitary. Climbs well. Eats insects, berries, seeds, hazelnuts and chestnuts. 8cm.

Long, fluffy tail

1cm
1.5cm
Fore foot   Hind foot

Black marks around eyes

Fore foot   1cm

Hind foot   1.5cm

⬅ Garden dormouse

Eats the same food and has the same habits as the common dormouse, but is larger, with a more pointed face. May enter buildings. Not found in Britain or Scandinavia. 13cm.

2cm
2.5cm
Fore foot   Hind foot

➡ European hamster

Lives on open grassland in Central Europe. Not found in Britain. Nocturnal. Lives on its own in a system of burrows. Hibernates. Stores food in its cheek pouches. 27cm.

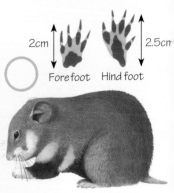

White cheeks and paws

Marmots and rats

➡ Alpine marmot

Families live in colonies in networks of long tunnels on the mountains of Europe. Not found in Britain. Active in the day. Has a waddling walk. Sits in an alert position and gives a warning whistle. Eats berries, seeds, nuts and insects. 55cm.

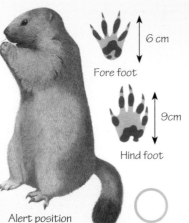

6 cm

Fore foot

9cm

Hind foot

Alert position

⬅ Common rat

Found worldwide. Lives in a colony, usually near houses. Makes a system of tunnels. Bold. Eats anything. 26cm.

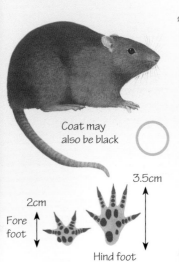

Coat may also be black

3.5cm

2cm

Fore foot

Hind foot

➡ Black rat / ship rat

Common near water, especially in ports and waterside buildings. Can climb well. Nocturnal and shyer than the common rat. Eats anything. 20cm.

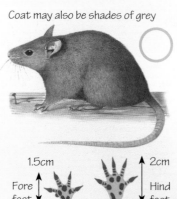

Coat may also be shades of grey

1.5cm

Fore foot

2cm

Hind foot

Voles and lemmings

➡ Water vole

Found near water all over Western Europe, except Ireland. Active by day. Swims well and digs burrows in the banks of ponds, canals, streams and marshes. Eats waterside plants and snails. 19cm.

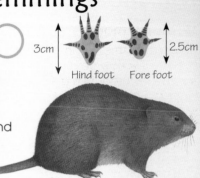

3cm
Hind foot

2.5cm
Fore foot

Coat may also be black

⬅ Short-tailed vole / field vole

Active by day. Makes tunnels below open ground. Not found in Ireland. Eats grass, leaves and moss. 11cm.

Short tail

1.2cm
Hind foot

1cm
Fore foot

➡ Bank vole

Widespread in deciduous woods and hedgerows. Active by day. Climbs well and makes its burrows in banks. Eats leaves, buds, berries and insects. 10cm.

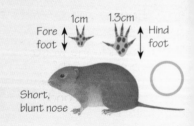

1cm
Fore foot

1.3cm
Hind foot

Short, blunt nose

⬅ Norway lemming

Lives in colonies, usually on mountains. Not found in Britain. Migrates in large groups every two or three years. Eats berries, grass and bark. 14cm.

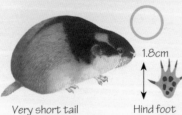

Very short tail

1.8cm
Hind foot

Mice

➡ House mouse

Found on farms and in buildings worldwide. Mostly nocturnal. Has a high squeak. Eats cereals, seeds, vegetables, fruit and stored fruit. 9cm.

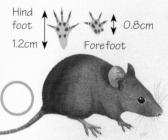

Hind foot 1.2cm

0.8cm Forefoot

Coat may also be black

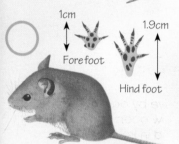

1cm Fore foot

1.9cm Hind foot

⬅ Wood mouse

Can be seen in gardens, hedgerows and woods. Digs burrows. Climbs and moves fast, making long leaps. Eats berries, buds, nuts, seeds and insects. 9cm.

➡ Yellow-necked field mouse

Similar habits to the wood mouse, but not usually found in the same areas. Lives in woodlands and may enter buildings. 10cm.

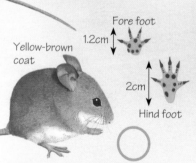

Fore foot 1.2cm

Yellow-brown coat

2cm Hind foot

⬅ Harvest mouse

Active by day. Good climber. Builds its breeding nests around corn and grass stalks. Eats soft leaves, insects and seeds. 6cm.

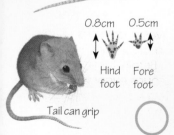

0.8cm Hind foot

0.5cm Fore foot

Tail can grip

Rabbits and hares

➡ Rabbit

Found on farmland, woodland, sand dunes, and hillsides. Lives in colonies in burrow systems. Active at dusk and dawn. Thumps the ground with its hind feet when alarmed. Eats grasses and plants. 40cm.

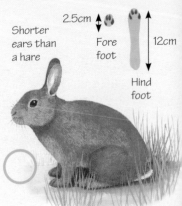

Shorter ears than a hare

2.5cm

Fore foot

12cm

Hind foot

Hind foot 13cm

3cm

Fore foot

Winter coat

Summer coat

⬅ Blue hare

Active by day and night. Rests above ground. Lives on its own. Found on heather moorland in Britain, Scandinavia and the Alps. Eats heather and grasses. 50cm.

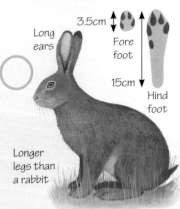

Long ears

3.5cm

Fore foot

15cm

Hind foot

Longer legs than a rabbit

➡ Brown hare

Usually solitary and silent. Rests above ground, in a hollow called a form. Lives in open farmland and woodland. Not found in Norway, Sweden, or most of Ireland. 58cm.

Seals

Long head

♀

Flipper

When a grey seal comes onto land, it usually rests on rocks, so you will not see any tracks

Coat is darker when wet

⬆ Grey seal

Found mostly along rocky shores of the British Atlantic coast and along the Baltic Sea. Lives in small herds. Voice is a drawn-out "coo-ee". Females give birth to a single pup. Eats mainly fish and crabs. 3m.

Drag mark

15cm

Fore foot

Fore foot

⬇ Common seal

Lives along the flat shores, estuaries, and mud-banks of the Scottish, eastern British, Danish, and Norwegian coasts. Usually silent, but may make a short bark. Females give birth to a single pup. Eats fish and shellfish. 1.5m.

Rounded head

Moles, hedgehogs and shrews

➡ Mole

Lives underground on farms and in woods. Not found in Ireland. Occasionally comes to the surface. Molehills are piles of waste earth from its tunnels. Sensitive to vibrations. Eats grubs, worms and insects. 13cm.

Short tail

Strong claws for digging

Fore foot 3.5cm

Hind foot 2cm

Hind foot   Fore foot

5cm   4cm

Prickles

Hair underneath

⬅ Hedgehog

Solitary and mainly nocturnal. Lives in ditches, hedgerows, parks and gardens. Spends winter hibernating. Makes snuffling, squealing, and snoring sounds. Rolls into a ball when alarmed. Eats worms and slugs. 25cm.

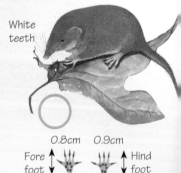

White teeth

Fore foot 0.8cm

Hind foot 0.9cm

➡ Millet's shrew

Found on the Channel Islands, and the Isles of Scilly. Lives in hedges, gardens, and the edges of woods. Very active and mainly nocturnal. Eats earthworms, insects and spiders. 8cm.

➡ Common shrew

Has a high, shrill squeak.
Can be aggressive.
Climbs and swims. Lives
in rough pasture, woods,
hedgerows, dunes, and
marshes. Not found in
Ireland. Eats insects
and worms. 7cm.

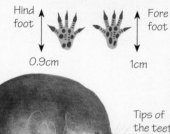

Hind foot 0.9cm

Fore foot 1cm

Tips of the teeth are red

Grey-white fur underneath

Fore foot 1.2cm

Hind foot 1.4cm

Velvety black fur on top

◀ Water shrew

Lives close to water; makes
tunnels in banks. A good
swimmer. Active by day and
night. Not found in Ireland.
Eats small fish, worms and
water insects. 8cm.

➡ Pygmy shrew

Habits and diet are
similar to those of
the common shrew.
Found in woods and
on grassland and
moorland. 5cm.

Pointed snout

Hind foot 0.5cm

Fore foot 0.4cm

Bats

➡ Pipistrelle bat

Rapid flight with jerky movements. Rusty to dark brown back, yellow-brown belly. Common in open woods, town parks and squares, and villages. Hibernates in a group in hollow trees and buildings. Wingspan 20cm; body length 5cm.

⬅ Long-eared bat

Yellow-brown back, paler belly. Not very common. Found in woodlands and orchards, and often near buildings. Flies in the late evening. Hibernates in cellars, caves and mine shafts. Ears fold up when at rest. Wingspan 25cm; body length 5cm.

➡ Daubenton's bat / water bat

May fly by day. Reddish-brown back, dirty white belly. Common in some places, usually near water. Large furry feet help to grab prey from the surface of water. Hibernates among rocks, cellars and roof-tops. Wingspan 24cm; body length 4cm.

➡ Noctule bat

Seen in parks, woods and gardens. Reddish-brown back, paler belly. Narrow wings and widely spaced ears. Hibernates in trees and buildings. Wingspan 38cm; body length 7cm.

⬅ Whiskered bat

Dark grey-brown back, greyish belly. Long body hair. Often seen flying low near water. Has a fluttering flight. Hibernates in trees, caves and cellars. Males usually solitary. Wingspan 23cm; body length 5cm.

➡ Greater horseshoe bat

Common in mountainous areas. Flies fairly low and may glide. Grey-brown back, pale grey belly. Male is a reddish colour. Broad wings, horseshoe-shaped nose. Hibernates in rocks, caves, quarries and mine shafts. Wingspan 35cm; body length 6cm.

Grebes, cormorants and herons

➡ Great crested grebe

Seen on open water, such as lakes and reservoirs. Sits low on the water and often dives. Builds a floating nest. Eats fish and water insects. 48cm.

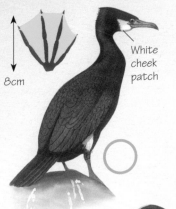

Crest expands during courtship display

White cheek patch

8cm

6cm

⬅ Cormorant

Perches upright, often with its wings spread out to dry. Found along coasts, usually on cliffs, sometimes on lake islands and rivers. May fly in flocks. Eats fish. 92cm.

➡ Grey heron

Stands motionless for long periods. Usually near water, by rivers, lakes, estuaries and marshes. Eats fish, frogs, voles, beetles and moles. 92cm.

Usually feeds by the bank, but may wade out into shallow water

12cm

Geese, ducks and pheasant

➡ Greylag goose

Nests on the ground in Scotland. Some breed further south. European birds may be seen near the coast. Lives in flocks which fly in a V formation. Eats grass and sometimes water plants. 82cm.

9cm

Pink legs

Male has a green head

♂

8cm

⬅ Mallard

Common on water. Female is mottled brown with a purple wing patch and greenish beak. Eats small water plants and sometimes water insects, snails and worms. 58cm.

9cm

➡ Pheasant

Lives on farmland with hedges. Often reared as game. Roosts in trees; nests on ground. Female is brown. Eats grain, insects and worms. Male 87cm; female 58cm.

Males can vary in colour and often have a white neck ring

♂

Moorhens, coots and curlews

➡ Moorhen

Seen swimming with a jerky movement on ponds, marshes and streams. Nests among reeds. Eats water plants, fruit, seeds, insects, worms and slugs. 33cm.

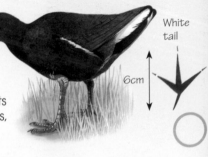

White tail

6cm

⬅ Coot

White forehead and beak

Usually found in groups on lakes and reservoirs. Bobs its head when swimming. Nests among reeds or water plants. Eats water plants and some insects. 38cm.

6cm

➡ Curlew

Very long, curved beak

8cm

Flies fast and high in large flocks. Found on mudflats, estuaries and coasts. Seen inland in summer. Eats insects, worms, berries, sea worms, crabs and small fish. 55cm.

Gulls, sparrows and rooks

➡ Herring gull

Most common gull on sea coasts; seen in ports and seaside towns. Nests on buildings and rocky cliffs. Feeds on shellfish, eggs, chicks, fish and food scraps scrounged from people. 56cm.

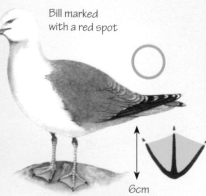

Bill marked with a red spot

6cm

2cm

Black bib

⬅ House sparrow

Lives on farmland, where it eats seeds, and in towns, where it feeds on scraps. May nest in buildings. Hops on the ground. Roosts in flocks. 15cm.

➡ Rook

Builds nests in groups called rookeries, usually in tall trees. Seen on farmland, often in flocks. Feeds on ploughed ground and eats insects, grubs and grain. 46cm.

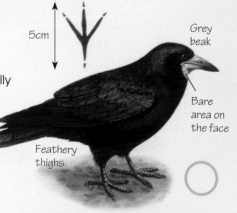

5cm

Grey beak

Bare area on the face

Feathery thighs

Insects

➡ Bark beetle

Bores into bark and makes a tunnel called a gallery, into which it lays eggs. On hatching, larvae bore side galleries of their own.

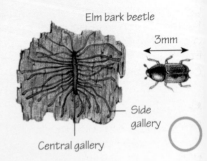

Elm bark beetle

3mm

Side gallery

Central gallery

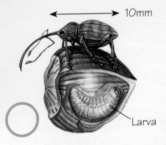

10mm

Larva

⬅ Nut weevil

Uses its long snout to drill into a hazelnut, then lays an egg inside. After larva hatches, it feeds on its hazelnut until autumn, when the nut falls to the ground. Larva then gnaws its way out.

⬇ Wood ant

Builds massive, cone-shaped nests from twigs and pine needles. Makes entrance holes in the roof, which it can close in cold weather.

8mm

Entrance holes

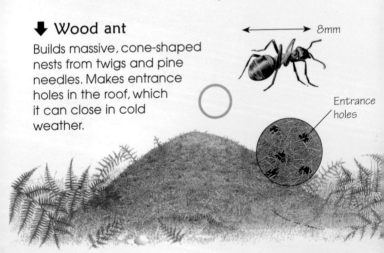

Galls

Galls are little growths produced by a tree in reaction to an irritation caused by a feeding larva. The gall grows around the larva, providing it with protection as it grows into an adult. Some galls house just one larva; others contain several, with each one inside its own chamber.

➡ Oak apple gall wasp

Females lay eggs on oak leaf buds. Red and green galls grow around larvae. Gall grows up to 4cm across and darkens as it ripens. Up to 30 larvae live inside a gall.

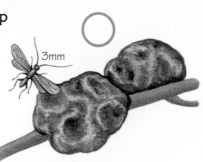

3mm

⬅ Oak marble gall wasp

Larva grows inside a gall on an oak leaf or twig. Galls are green in summer; later ripen to brown, and stay on the branches throughout winter.

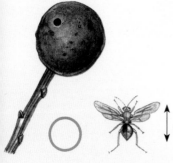

4mm

➡ Aphid

Cause pineapple-shaped galls to grow on spruce trees. In August, the galls break open, dry up and turn brown.

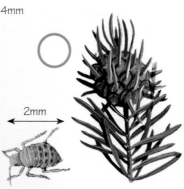

2mm

Mammal skulls

As you look for tracks and signs, you could find the bones of a dead animal. You might be able to identify what type of animal it is by looking closely at its skull.

➡ Mole

Insect-eater. Notice the long muzzle and the sharp teeth used for chewing hard insect bodies. The skull may be inside owl pellets.

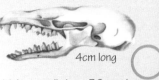

Moles usually have 36 teeth

⬅ Grey squirrel

Plant-eater. Has strong front incisor teeth used for gnawing and biting hard plant material.

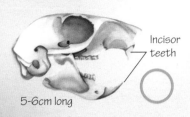

Incisor teeth

5-6cm long

➡ Badger

Meat-eater. Notice the long canine teeth and sharp chewing teeth for tearing and chewing meat. Strong jaw muscles are attached to the ridge on top of the skull.

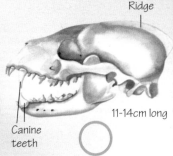

Ridge

Canine teeth

11-14cm long

⬅ Roe deer

Plant-eater. Has long incisor teeth on lower jaw used for biting off bits of plants, and flat molar teeth for chewing them.

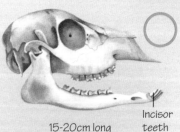

15-20cm long

Incisor teeth

Bird beaks

If you find a bird skull, the shape of the beak will give you clues to what sort of food the bird ate.

Stong, short beak

⬆ Hawfinch

Seed-eater. Finches have strong, stubby beaks used for cracking open seeds and nuts.

Strong, chisel-like beak

⬆ Oystercatcher

Feeds on animals that live in mud. Has a long, powerful beak that can probe for and prise open shells.

Flat beak

⬆ Mallard

Tiny plants and animals are caught in grooves on the beak as water is passed through its bill.

Sharp, hooked beak

⬆ Tawny owl

Meat-eater. All owls use their hooked beaks to tear meat.

Sharp, stabbing beak

⬆ Green woodpecker

Insect-eater. Has a long, sharp, strong beak to probe for and pick up insects, and to chip wood.

Sharp, dagger-like beak

⬆ Reed warbler

Insect-eater. Uses its thin, pointed beak to catch flying insects.

Long, stabbing beak

⬆ Grey heron

Fish-eater. Has a long, sharp beak used for stabbing fish and water animals.

39

Fur and feathers

Fur and hairs

Bits of fur or hair can be found in places where an animal has had to squeeze through or under something, usually wood or barbed wire. Fur on the ground may be a sign of a fight or the remains of an animal's meal.

⬇ Sheep wool

Usually found on barbed wire. Often in matted lumps.

⬆ Badger hairs

Badgers tend to follow regular pathways. Where these pass under fences, loo for hairs stuck to the wood.

Feathers

All birds shed old and worn out feathers, so feathers are usually easy to find, even in the busiest cities. Here are some of the types of feathers you might see.

Jay's wing feather

Pheasant's tail feather

Wood pigeon's wing feather

Mallard's wing feather

Pheasant's body feather

Meal remains of predators

Most animals eaten by predators are small, and so are gobbled down whole. If a predator is disturbed while it eats, it may leave remains of its meal. Some deliberately leave a part of their food if it is inedible, or they may store it for later.

Beetle

↑ Stored food

Shrikes store food, such as insects, mice, lizards and small birds, by pinning it onto branches and barbed wire.

↑ Pierced eggs

Beech martens bite a hole in a bird's egg to reach the food inside.

↑ Fish remains

Otters may leave remains of fish near water. They often eat the head first.

↑ Small birds

Many birds of prey eat smaller birds. They usually tear off the head, pluck out the feathers and peck at the flesh.

↑ Smashed snail shells

Song thrushes smash snail shells open on rocks, leaving bits of shell.

Meal remains of plant-eaters

Plant-eating animals, such as birds and rodents, leave signs of feeding in different parts of a plant. Look for marks in leaves, buds, fruit and even in bark.

⬆ Bark

Deer, squirrels and voles tear strips of bark off tree trunks, leaving teeth marks. Deer leave the biggest marks.

Pecked by sparrow

Chewed by bank vole

⬆ Young plants

Look for young plants in spring. Birds peck at leaves and flowers. Voles chew shoots, leaving tooth marks.

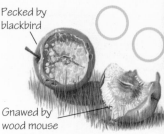

Pecked by blackbird

Gnawed by wood mouse

⬆ Fallen fruit

Look for teeth marks made by rodents near the edge of the skin. Birds leave peck marks in the flesh.

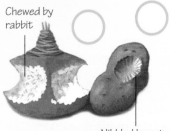

Chewed by rabbit

Nibbled by rat

⬆ Root crops

Rats and voles gnaw at roots above and below ground. Hares, rabbits, and deer eat the parts above ground.

Gnawed by squirrel

⬆ Fungi

Look on the flesh for teeth marks made by rodents. Slugs leave small, round holes on the surface.

Cones eaten by animals

Cones grow on conifer trees. They contain seeds, which are protected by tough scales. To get to the seeds, birds have to lift, tear or pull back the scales. Rodents gnaw at the cones, usually starting by chewing off the larger scales at the top.

⬇ Signs of squirrels
Scales are removed, leaving a rough stem.

Pine cone gnawed by squirrel

⬇ Signs of crossbills
Scales are either pushed out or split.

Pine cone pecked by crossbill

⬇ Signs of wood mice
Scales are gnawed off close to the stem.

Pine cone nibbled by wood mouse

⬇ Signs of woodpeckers
Scales are pecked, giving them a messy appearance.

Pine cone pecked by woodpecker

43

Nuts eaten by animals

In autumn, look under trees and bushes that produce nuts, such as hazel bushes, and chestnut, walnut and beech trees. If you find nut shells, look for teeth or beak marks, and notice the shape and edge of the hole made by the animal. Each type of animal has its own particular way of eating a nut.

⬇ Signs of rats and squirrels

Shells are split and gnawed.

Walnut chewed by rat

Hazelnut split and nibbled by grey squirrel

⬇ Signs of hawfinches

Stones cracked open, usually split in half.

Cherry stones

⬇ Signs of woodpeckers

Nuts usually found wedged into cracks in bark. Shattered with several blows of the bird's beak.

Almond

Beechnut

Hazelnut

⬇ Signs of rabbits

Long front teeth leave scrape marks.

Sweet chestnut

Acorn

⬇ Signs of tits

Jagged holes where the birds have chipped away at the shells.

Walnut pecked at by blue tit

Walnut eaten by great tit

Hazelnut chipped by great tit

⬇ Signs of wood mice

Look for teeth marks around the hole.

Hazelnut   Cherry stone

Beechnut

Acorn   Almond kernel

⬇ Signs of voles and dormice

Leave smooth-edged holes, usually in base of nut.

Hazelnut eaten by dormouse

Hazelnut gnawed by bank vole

45

Mammal droppings

Droppings are mostly made of parts of food that an animal can't digest, such as bones, tough seeds, plant fibres, and hard parts of insects. Meat-eaters leave sausage-shaped droppings with pointed ends; plant-eaters usually leave small, round droppings. Remember never to touch the droppings you might find.

0.8-1.2cm

Group of droppings stuck together

1-1.5cm

↑ Fallow deer

Made up of plant fibres. In summer, often soft and may stick together.

1-1.4cm

0.7-1cm

↑ Roe deer

May be found singly or in heaps, sometimes stuck together. Very round in winter.

1cm

↑ Rabbit

Used to mark territory. Usually in piles, often near burrows, sometimes on heaps of earth, clumps of grass, ant hills or tree stumps.

1.5-2cm

↑ Hare

Pale brown in winter, dark brown in summer. Flatter than rabbit droppings. Left where the hare has been feeding or near its home.

46

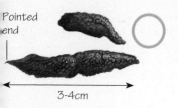

Pointed
end

3-4cm

↑ Hedgehog

Often contains hard parts of
insects, such as fragments
of beetle wings. Can also
be made up of fur, bones,
feathers and berries.

7-10cm

↑ Fox

Left outside the den, or on
rocks or clumps of grass.
Twisted at one end. Might
contain bits of mice, birds,
insects, fruit, seeds or berries.

May be oval-shaped
or semi-liquid

10cm

↑ Badger

Left in specially dug holes,
about 10cm deep. Unlike
cats, badgers don't cover
their droppings.

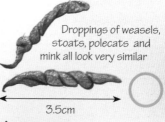

Droppings of weasels,
stoats, polecats and
mink all look very similar

3.5cm

↑ Weasel

Narrow and twisted. Often
left on rocks or clumps
of grass. May contain fur,
bones and feathers.

Look similar
to mouse
droppings

← 0.6cm →

↑ Field vole

Greenish or brown with a
smooth edge. Made up of
plant remains.

Droppings of black
rat are shorter
and thinner
than brown rat
droppings.

← 1.7cm →

↑ Brown rat

Left singly or in piles. Made
up of plant remains. Usually
dark brown or black.

Bird pellets and droppings

Pellets

Some birds swallow their food whole, then cough up pellets of the parts they can't digest. These parcels can be made up of fur, bones, feathers or insect parts. Look for them in places where birds feed, roost and nest, but remember never to touch pellets with your bare hands.

⬇ Gull pellets

Loose pellets often made up of fish bones and plant remains. Look near water.

3.5-6cm

⬇ Crow pellets

Found in fields and other feeding places. Often made up of grit and plant remains.

3-4.5cm

⬇ Rook pellets

May contain grit and plant remains. Look under nests.

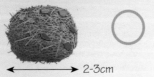

2-3cm

⬇ Birds of prey pellets

Can be found under perching spots, such as fences, tree stumps or tall trees. The birds don't swallow bones, so they are not present in their pellets.

Kestrel pellet showing mammal fur

1.5-2cm

3-5.5cm

Sparrowhawk pellet showing bird feathers

1-2cm

2-4cm

Common buzzard pellet showing mammal fur

2.5-3cm

6-7cm

↓ Owl pellets

Can be found under owls' perching or nesting spots such as posts, branches, barns and holes in trees.

Short-eared owl pellet showing bird feathers and bones

←——— 4-9cm ———→

Little owl pellet showing bird bones and feathers, and insect remains

←—— 2.5cm ——→

Tawny owl pellet showing bird feathers and bones

←——— 4-7cm ———→

Barn owl pellet showing mammal fur and bones, and bird bones

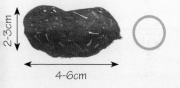

2-3cm ↕   ←——— 4-6cm ———→

Droppings

Birds that don't produce pellets get rid of any food they can't digest, such as seeds and berries, in droppings. Droppings come in three types: liquid, semi-firm and round, and firm and long.

↑ Starling droppings

White liquid. Can be found at feeding and roosting sites, and under nests.

↑ Pheasant droppings

Colour varies, but usually has white urine at one end. Semi-firm. 2cm long.

↑ Goose droppings

Green or grey-brown. Made up of plant material. Firm. 5-8cm long.

Mammal homes

Below ground

Outside the entrance to its burrow, an animal might leave signs, such as droppings or tracks. The size of the entrance might also tell you what kind of animal lives inside. Spider webs across a hole tells you that the burrow is not being used.

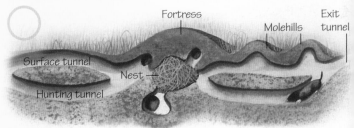

Fortress

Molehills

Exit tunnel

Surface tunnel

Nest

Hunting tunnel

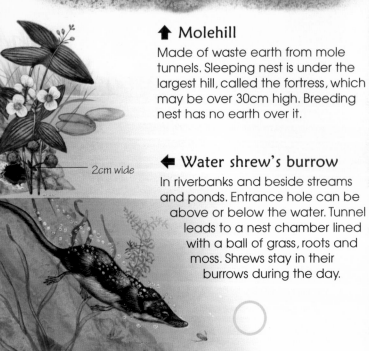

2cm wide

⬆ Molehill

Made of waste earth from mole tunnels. Sleeping nest is under the largest hill, called the fortress, which may be over 30cm high. Breeding nest has no earth over it.

⬅ Water shrew's burrow

In riverbanks and beside streams and ponds. Entrance hole can be above or below the water. Tunnel leads to a nest chamber lined with a ball of grass, roots and moss. Shrews stay in their burrows during the day.

Breeding hole entrance covered with earth

Earth from the burrow

Sleeping chamber

↑ Rabbit warren

Lots of entrance holes and many tunnels. Rabbits live together in groups. Holes dug from the outside have piles of earth outside them. Can be shallow hollows nearby and droppings near the holes.

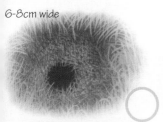

6-8cm wide

← Water vole's burrow

Entrance hole just above water in the soft banks of rivers and streams. Voles usually eat the plants around the hole.

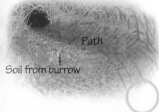

3-4cm wide

Path

Soil from burrow

← Wood mouse's burrow

In woods and hedgerows. Look for a well-trodden path and a mound of soil outside the entrance. Wood mice spend their days in their burrows.

6-8cm wide

Path

Soil from burrow

← Rat's burrow

Rats can burrow in almost any soil or compost heaps. Each burrow has two holes – one main entrance and one emergency exit.

Mammal homes

Above ground

Some mammals, such as deer, don't have fixed homes, but sleep on bare patches of ground. Others build nests. You might see the nests in winter, when trees are bare and grasses have died away. It's important never to disturb a nest, otherwise the animal might abandon it.

➡ Grey squirrel's drey

20-50c wide

Made of twigs, lined with moss, grass, feathers and fur. Looks like a round bird's nest in the fork of a tree or on a side branch.

8-10cm wide

⬅ Harvest mouse's summer nest

Made of grass leaves woven around long grass or reed stems, high off the ground, sometimes in bushes.

➡ Dormouse's winter nest

8cm wide

Made of plant material, mainly strips of bark. Found in undergrowth, often close to the ground, or in bushes and bird nesting boxes.

40cm long

⬅ Hare's form

A shallow hollow scraped away in earth, grass or snow usually protected at the side by a clump of grass or a stone. Hare sits with its hindquarters in the form.

Bird nests

Birds usually build nests in spring and summer in places that are well hidden or difficult to reach – high up in trees, on water, or in a hole. You can look for nests in winter, when there is less cover. Nests must never be touched – even ones that look abandoned could be used again the next year. In many countries, it's illegal to disturb a bird's nest.

➡ Lesser black-backed gull nest

Shallow hole in ground lined with plant material. On cliffs, stony beaches or moors. Eggs camouflaged to blend in with rocky surroundings. May to June.

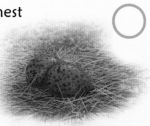

⬅ Woodpecker nest

Bird makes hole in tree and builds nest inside. Hole about 38cm deep. You may see wood chips underneath. April to May.

➡ Swallow nest

High off the ground, stuck to a surface, usually on a wall. Made of mud and bits of plants, lined with feathers. May to June.

⬅ Wren nest

Oval nest made of feathers, grass and moss. Well hidden in undergrowth, under leaves, or in holes in trees, banks or walls. April to June.

Bird nests

➡ Long-tailed tit nest

Large, egg-shaped nest
well hidden in scrub,
hedges, brambles or gorse.
Occasionally in trees.
Made of moss and lichen
woven with hairs and
spiders' webs. Lined with
feathers. March to April.

⬅ Rook nest

Rooks breed in colonies
called rookeries. Nest built in
tree tops, and made of stick
and earth. Lined with bits of
plants, wool and hair. Same
nest may be used year
after year. Can be used for
roosting. March to May.

➡ Song thrush nest

Nest is 1.5-3.5m off the
ground, hidden in hedges,
shrubs or trees, usually close
to the trunk. Made of twigs,
roots, grass, lichen and
dead leaves. Lined with
mud. March to June.

⬅ Coot nest

Built among water plants
in or near water on lakes,
ponds and streams. Made
of stems of water plants
and dead leaves. March
to April.

Spider webs

7-18mm

➡ Garden spider / cross spider

Spins circular web with threads in a spiral pattern. Hangs, head down, in centre of web. Waits motionless for insects to become caught in the sticky threads.

⬅ House spider

Spins untidy, sheet web in corners of houses and sheds. Web has a funnel-shaped part in which the spider hides.

➡ Money spider

Has horizontal sheet web, attached to long grass or twigs by tangled strands. Insects fly into the strands and drop onto the sheet. Spider then runs underneath the sheet, and bites the prey through the web.

9-14mm

2mm

⬅ Wall spider

Makes tube-like web in cracks in walls, then hides underneath. Webs have tripwire threads sticking out. When an insect touches a tripwire thread, the web trembles and the spider dashes out to grab its prey.

2-3mm

55

Taking pictures

If you want to keep a record of the tracks and signs you've seen, you can take a camera out spotting with you and photograph your finds. Here are a few tips on how to take a good picture of a track or sign:

• Keep the Sun behind you and make sure your shadow doesn't fall across your subject as you're taking the photo.

• If there isn't much light you may need to use the camera's flash.

• If your subject is difficult to see amongst leaves or grass, place a piece of card behind it to make a plain background.

• If you don't have a ruler to measure the track or sign, you can photograph an object, such as a coin, next to it to show how big it is.

You could use your camera's zoom function to take close-up pictures of tiny things, like this garden spider on its web.

Useful words

These pages explain some specialist words you might come across when reading about flowers, trees, birds and insects. Words that are written in *italic text* are defined separately.

algae – tiny, simple, rootless plants that live in water

antlers – bony extensions that grow from the head of members of the deer family

bank – sloping land beside a lake, river or stream

bark – a tough outer layer that protects a tree's insides

bill – another word for beak

bird of prey – a bird that hunts other animals for food

breed – (1) a variety of animal within a *species* that has ancestors and distinguishing characteristics in common, for example Jersey cows (2) to produce young

bud – an undeveloped *shoot*, *leaf* or *flower*

burrow – a hole in the ground made by an animal for shelter

camouflage – when an animal or object's colour makes it difficult to see against certain backgrounds

coat – a growth of hair, wool or fur covering an animal's body

colony – a group of animals of the same *species* living together

cones – the *fruits* of *conifers*

conifer – a tree with needle-like or scaly *leaves*, which bears *cones* with their *seeds* inside. Most conifers are *evergreen*.

copse – a small, low woodland

cover – anywhere that animals hide themselves, for example hedges, bushes or thick grass

crest – a showy growth of feathers on a bird's head

deciduous – a tree that loses its *leaves* over a few weeks, usually in autumn

domesticated – kept by people

droppings – bird or animal poo

estuary – the place where a large river meets the sea

evergreen – a tree that loses its *leaves* throughout the year, so it is always green

fawn – a young deer

fern – a flowerless plant that has fronds instead of *leaves* and spores instead of *seeds*

flock – a group of animals

flower – the part of a plant where new *seeds* are made

fore foot – the front foot of a four-legged animal

fruits – the parts of a plant that hold its *seeds*

fungi (singular: **fungus**) – simple, plant-like living things that typically feed off dead or living animals and plants

gall – a swelling of plant tissue caused by insects feeding

game – a bird that is hunted by people for food or sport

herd – a group of *mammals* that live together

hibernation – the sleepy state in which some animals spend winter

hind foot – the back foot of a four-legged animal

hoof – the hard, horny casing covering the toes or lower part of the foot of certain *mammals*

larva (plural: **larvae**) – the young stage of an insect which is very different from the adult insect, e.g. a caterpillar is a larva of a butterfly

leaf – flat, thin growth from a plant's *stem* that is usually green. Leaves make food for the plant.

lichen – *algae* and *fungi* growing together

mammal – a warm-blooded animal that has hair and feeds its young with milk

migrant – an animal that *migrate.*

migrate – when an animal breeds in one area, then moves to another for the winter, returning again the following spring

moor – an open area of land tha is wet and windy

muzzle – the pointed part of the head of some *mammals*, including the nose and jaw

native – originally coming from

nocturnal – active at night

omnivore – an animal that eats plants and other animals

pad – the fleshy cushion-like underside of an animal's toes

pasture – a grassland used to provide food for farm animals

pellet – a small parcel of undigested food that has been coughed up by a bird

perch – (1) when a bird stands or a branch or other resting place by gripping with its toes (2) the place where a bird perches

predator – an animal that kills and eats other animals

prey – an animal that is hunted by another animal for food

rodent – a small *mammal* that has two pairs of constantly growing teeth used for gnawing

roost – when a bird sleeps

roots – parts of a plant that grow into the ground, absorbing water and goodness from the soil and anchoring the plant

sand dune – a mound or ridge of sand created when dune grasses trap sand grains being blown by the wind

scales – the tough, woody parts of a *cone*

scavenger – an animal that feeds on waste and the dead bodies of animals

scrub – an area of land covered with grasses, herbs and low shrubs

seed – part of a flowering plant that may grow into a new plant

shoot – a young *stem* or twig bearing *leaves*

species – a group of plants or animals that all look alike, behave in the same way and can breed together

stalk – a slender *stem* that supports a *leaf* and attaches it to a larger stem of a plant

stem – the part of a plant that supports the *leaves* and *flowers*, and carries water and food around the plant

solitary – living alone

territory – the area defended by an animal, or pair of animals, for *breeding*

track – an animal's footprint

trail – a series of *tracks* made by a moving animal

trunk – the main woody *stem* of the tree that holds it upright

tundra – a frozen, treeless area in which only small shrubs, mosses and *lichens* can grow

undergrowth – small trees, bushes and plants growing beneath taller trees in a wood or forest

urine – bird or animal wee

waterfowl – birds that spend a lot of time on water

web – a net-like structure of sticky silk threads made by a spider for catching insects

webbing – flaps of skin connecting the toes of some water birds and mammals

Scorecard

When you start spotting, you'll soon find that some animals and their signs are rarer than others. To give you a rough idea of how likely you are to see them, all the birds, mammals, insects and signs in the book are listed here with a score next to each one.

Common species score 5 points; rare ones are worth 25. Species are listed alphabetically. Where this book gives an alternative name, look up the first name that appears. If you want to, you can use the "Date spotted" boxes to record when you saw each species.

Animals

Species	Score	Date spotted	Species	Score	Date spotted
Alpine marmot	25		Common dormouse	20	
Aphid	5		Common rat	5	
Arctic fox	25		Common seal	10	
Badger	15		Common shrew	10	
Bank vole	10		Coot	5	
Bark beetle	15		Cormorant	10	
Beaver	25		Coypu	20	
Beech marten	25		Curlew	15	
Black rat / ship rat	25		Daubenton's bat / water bat	15	
Blue hare	15		Domestic cat	5	
Brown bear	25		Domestic cow	5	
Brown hare	5		Domestic dog	5	
Chamois	25		Domestic goat	10	

Species	Score	Date spotted	Species	Score	Date spotted
Domestic pig	5		Mallard	5	
Domestic sheep	5		Millet's shrew	25	
Edible dormouse	20		Mole	10	
Elk / moose	25		Moorhen	5	
European hamster	25		Mouflon / wild sheep	25	
European mink	15		Muntjac	20	
Exmoor pony	10		Muskrat	25	
Fallow deer	10		Noctule bat	10	
Garden dormouse	25		Norway lemming	25	
Great crested grebe	20		Nut weevil	5	
Greater horseshoe bat	20		Oak apple gall wasp	5	
Grey heron	15		Oak marble gall wasp	5	
Greylag goose	15		Otter	20	
Grey seal	15		Pheasant	10	
Grey squirrel	5		Pine marten	20	
Harvest mouse	20		Pipistrelle bat	10	
Hedgehog	10		Polecat	20	
Herring gull	5		Pygmy shrew	15	
House mouse	5		Rabbit	5	
House sparrow	5		Red deer	15	
Ibex / wild goat	25		Red fox	10	
Long-eared bat	15		Red squirrel	15	
Lynx	25		Reindeer	15	

Species	Score	Date spotted	Species	Score	Date spotted
Roe deer	15		Whiskered bat	15	
Rook	5		Wild boar	25	
Short-tailed vole / field vole	5		Wild cat	20	
Sika deer	15		Wolf	25	
Stoat	15		Wood ant	10	
Water shrew	15		Wood mouse	10	
Water vole	15		Yellow-necked field mouse	15	
Weasel	15				

Animal signs

Species	Score	Date spotted	Species	Score	Date spotted
Bird beaks	20		Mammal droppings	5	
Bird droppings	5		Mammal homes above ground	20	
Bird nests	10		Mammal homes below ground	10	
Bird pellets	20		Mammal skulls	20	
Cones eaten by animals	15		Meal remains of plant-eaters	15	
Feathers	5		Meal remains of predators	25	
Fur	5		Nuts eaten by animals	15	
Galls	5		Spider webs	5	

Index

Edited by Sarah Khan
Designed by Stephanie Jones and Joanne Kirkby
Digital manipulation by Keith Furnival and Mike Olley

Additional illustrations by Graham Allen, Dave Ashby, Bob Bampton,
John Barber, Derick Bown, Roger H Coggins, Denise Finney, Sheila
Galbraith, Christine Howes, Ian Jackson, Andy Martin, Annabel Milne,
Robert Morton, Tricia Newell, Richard Orr, Peter Stebbing, David Wright
and others

PHOTO CREDITS: Cover © Edwin Giesbers / Foto Natura / Minden
Pictures / Getty Images; 1 © Tom Brakefield / CORBIS; 2 and 3 © David
Tipling / Alamy; 7 © Papilio / Alamy; 8 © DAVID TIPLING / naturepl.com;
56 © blickwinkel / Alamy